# *Contents*

# REALIZATION

# RESPECT

# COURAGE TO BELIEVE

*Dedication*

*I dedicate this book to my Lord and Savior Jesus Christ for calling me into, and equipping me for the ministry of poetry. Second, to my late, great parents: the Reverend Robert Lee White and Melissa "Mabel" Gilchrist-White for teaching me how to be as great as God created me to be, without fear or regret. Last, to my late grandfather, Robert Lee Gilchrist, who passed while this project was coming to a close for helping me to be all God is calling me to be.*

*Acknowledgments*

*Truly I tell you, just as you did it to one of the least of these who are members of my family, you did it to me*
—*Matthew 25:40*[1]

I extend appreciation:

To my first friend, my best friend, my sister Bridgette for being my everything. To my family, immediate and extended, for teaching me how to be who I am perfectly.

To the team responsible for Spiritual Metamorphosis: Reverend Dr. Joseph W. Daniels, Mama Velma Falby, and Sister Joan Ventour, for agreeing to serve as my Spiritual Leaders. To Donna Cypress, Allison Poinsett, and Shirley Avery, for being meticulous editors. To Illustrator T.W. Martin, for allowing God to use you artistically.

To my church family at Emory United Methodist Church for your prayers, contributions, cheers, tears, and unconditional love. It is a blessing to be in a fellowship where the Holy Spirit is present on a full time basis.

To my many, wonderful friends who have truly been sources of encouragement since the onset of the project.

And to everyone who is reading this book. I pray that it is as much, if not more, of a blessing to you as it has been for me to create.

# Introduction to
## *Spiritual Metamorphosis*

*Do not hide your light under a basket! Instead, put it on a
stand and let it shine for all that they may glorify God
—Matthew 5:15[1]*

Over the course of my life, God has blessed me to encounter a
myriad of experiences: some negative, others positive, but all
instrumental in helping me to become the person God is calling
me to be. Spiritual Metamorphosis captures the many experiences
one may encounter when walking in relationship with Christ. Many
of the poems in this text reflect my personal experiences, lessons
learned, and the spiritual growth I have been fortunate enough to
acquire.

The term metamorphosis[2] means a change in form and habit.
God sent experiences my way and God allowed me to be changed
by them in a positive manner. While I may not have understood,
the Creator knew that good would arise from every situation.
Jeremiah 29: 11[3] reads, "For surely I know the plans I have for
you, says the Lord, plans for your welfare and not for harm, to give
you a future with hope." It was difficult for me to see God's welfare

in being molested at the age of five. However, this experience allowed me to take a formative stand against violating a minor's sexuality, thus the Holy Spirit led me to make a conscious decision never to violate another person in such a manner. Rather than hate the person who inflicted such pain upon me, God allowed me to understand his pain, forgive him, and love him for who he is unconditionally.

It was not until I was into my twenties that the event caused me to question some of the choices I made in my life. I believe that even the effort I make to understand my journey is a part of God's plan for my welfare. On the contrary, I have not always made wise decisions. I repeatedly placed myself in jeopardy. All the while, God thought enough of me to give me second chances. When I sit and reflect on God's goodness, my repeated mistakes, and the point at which I realized my faults, it is easy for me to detect my spiritual growth.

As a woman of God, I think it robbery to sit on God's goodness. Goodness, in this sense, does not mean free of difficulty; it means that in the hands of all things great and small lie the hands of the Creator. I believe that each of us are endowed with a "light" as stated in Matthew 5:15. My light is the gift of poetry and public speaking. From great pain, comes great progress. I feel I have endured my share of pain. In this I find comfort, for often when I am wounded God anoints me with a poem to soothe my pain; to give clarity to the event's significance in my life. As human beings, our reactions to situations differ. I find myself at peace when I am able to write or talk. God has bestowed these gifts upon me. My mother used to tell me, "When God gives you a talent and you don't use it, God will take it away." In this instance, I am glad God sent people along to encourage me to bring forth this book.

I have been growing in the field of poetic writing since seventh grade when I used to copy, cut, and paste published poets' works together. At that time, I wanted to impress a young man. What began as a gesture to gain personal attention transformed into spiritual motivation. God took me from being an imitator of human kind to being an originator in that I write to glorify Christ, my

Lord and Savior. Therefore, I abide in the spirit in regards to my writings for I know this is where I am made complete.

As I continue on this journey, I find peace in knowing that there is nothing to great for God. You will discover four sections in the text: Conflicts, Realization, Respect, and Courage to Believe. The sections coexist with one another. For growth from a conflict is not possible without realizing that there is something valuable to be gained. Once we reach the point of realization, we are able to give, demand and accept that which we deny ourselves, respect. In addition, when we feel respected, it is easier for us to have the courage to believe. Indeed there is a change in form, habits, and actions/reactions that take place throughout the book; a change which can only be brought on by the presence of the Holy Spirit.

You will find an array of subjects covered in Spiritual Metamorphosis. I speak to the outcast of the world in poems such as "We Da Havenots" and "Isms." In other poems, I share common emotions as they pertain to being in relationship with God: "Just As I Am," "Unworthy," and "God Gave Me The Wind." There are poems that convey the importance of faith, community ties, and the blessings of a mother. Included are pieces that speak to the troubled at heart and poems that will make you laugh. I am grateful for the exposure I have received over the course of my life; all are working together for the purpose of this book which is to illustrate how God transforms.

I pray that your soul is awakened, that you find peace in being the person God is calling you to be. Today is your day!

God bless,

Roberta Sonsaray White
December 12, 2003

# CONFLICTS

*Galatians 5[1]*

[16] So I say, live by the Spirit, and you will not gratify the desires of the sinful nature. [17] For the sinful nature desires what is contrary to the Spirit, and the Spirit what is contrary to the sinful nature. They are in conflict with each other, so that you do not do what you want. [18] But if you are led by the Spirit, you are not under law.

What is it that ails you? Who is it that angers you? Why do you insist on living your way? The answer: The force that diverts our attention from God is the result of an inner conflict between Spirit and worldly self.

Many, on the road of spiritual maturity which is a life long journey, have experienced the war of choices: Spirit vs. sin. Several of us travel between the two extremities in search of wholeness. Some of us are fortunate enough to have a personal encounter with the Holy Spirit. This meeting of Spirit and flesh alters our approach to life altogether. Depending on our circumstance, our pivotal point varies. However, when we walk on the road to spiritual maturity, eventually we choose the greater of the two: Spirit. On the contrary, some of us insist on abiding in sin. In this vain the consequence is spiritual and physical death; a journey of temporary gratification.

In this section, you will read twenty-five poems that speak to the inner conflicts inhabited by people called by God. The works are arranged to expose you to various areas of concern that reside inside of us before and after we decide to walk with Christ.

## Jonah 3[2]

[8] . . . Everyone must turn from their evil ways and stop all their violence.

# *Follow Your Dreams*

My heart tells me to fly, but fear keeps me standing still
I want to be the very best, I long to do God's will
So why am I sitting here with this pencil in my hand
when my heart is telling me to write
God's glory, tell my story and follow The Divine Plan
Today I will take one step closer to my calling
I will begin working on my story
I now accept my calling.

R.S. White
9-9-02

# *Where Does Your Faith Lay?*

Seeping, sinking, way down low
Beaten, bitten, life deals hard blows
Kicked, slapped, pushed aside.
Now tell me where does your faith lay?

Do you feel as if this is it?
Do you ask why all these hits?
Do you feel as if you are the chosen one?
Now tell me where does your faith lay?

Have you gambled all your rent money or
sacrificed your soul for silver and gold?
Selfish, senseless, living on the edge;
Now you ask" Does God care?"
God cares, and always has
But Satan had you convinced that you no longer had a Dad
The same Creator who commanded,
"Cast your cares upon me for I care for you"
Longs to forgive for you are His
Chosen One

Now get down on your knees and make a solemn plea
Put a period on this part of your life
And keep on moving.

Roberta S. White

# *Selective Spirit*

In the word it says, "God has not given us the spirit of fear"
Yet every time we cross paths you walk by as if I am not near
You look in my direction with such a warm grin,
and when I turn 'round
I realize you are smiling at your friend.

Some days I am deep in spiritually broken pain
Yet when I enter the sanctuary broken I often leave the same
After the final "Amen" of the pastor
You lift your head from prayer
Then like before, yes once more, you by pass me
for the exit door.

We cross paths on Tuesday during a committee meeting
You walk in, smile, yet you never, ever greet anyone.

Roberta S. White
6-22-02

# The Loudest Cry Is the Cry
# No One Hears

The loudest cry is the cry no one hears
It is an internal moaning
That creeks, and squeaks like ungreased
Tires, with brakes that pull and tug
Like weights attached to the bottom of roller
Skates sinking to the bottom of the ocean;
An ocean without a bottom

The loudest cry is the cry encouraged by discouragement
It lives inside one's body
When others voice their doubts,
It tells the person his dreams are illusions;
It shoots down the lady who dreams of ways
to teach our children
Herstory for history does not include you and I
And most of what is written is a slave owner's descendants' lies.

The loudest cry is the cry of sin
That waits outside the door of the rich and the poor
Ready to snag
God's creation from fulfilling his purpose;
Sin can wear a stylish mini skirt, can be a married woman or
divorced man,
An attorney, doctor, or preacher man.
Sin seeks to devour the soul,
Not in parts, but whole
Taking from within what was once labeled
"God's reward."

The loudest cry is the cry with no tears
But is accompanied by fears of living, survival, and
The possibility of success
The cry eeks like a rusty nail scrapping
Glass, leaving deep lines
And cracks that symbolize defeat,
Failure, and lack;
It is the yin without the yang;
The night without darkness or cold freezing rain;
It is bitter and mean

No one ever ponders tears unseen
For the loudest cry is the cry no one hears.

R.S. White
1-27-02

# God Bless'd or Tested it

*Jesus loves me this I know*
*For my mother often told me so*
*Pastor led me to God's word*
*And often times I've heard*
*From the Master through the voices of others*
*Tried and true.*
*Yet I often wonder why God*
*Takes me through challenges and tests*
*If I am "blessed"*
*Why do I feel like such a mess?*

*Lord God You put Your trust in me*
*And once again I sinned against You*
*Please believe me when I say*
*I never meant to dismiss You*

*My weaknesses . . .*
*Are they tests or blessings or blessings within a test?*
*Dear God my heart is with You but my head is such a mess.*

*You've given me a spirit of discernment*
*And I realize my actions*
*Are unjust*
*But if You would, please*
*Forgive me once more and continue*
*To trust in me*

*Lord, I'm so alone*
*Never thought I could be this simple:*
*Repeating the same mistake infinite square*
*Failing to acknowledge my blessings:*
*Beautiful eyes, spirit, and hair; settling for praises*
*Of beauty from a non-believer*
*Why must I experience such bitter evil?*

*Help me to learn from my experiences*
*My prayer is for a blessing from this test.*

R.S. White
2-6-02

# *Nobody Owes You*

When the world falls beneath your feet
And the hills seem to slope instead of descend . . .
Remember that Nobody Owes you Nothing

*Double negatives such a sin*
Holding people accountable will never permit you to win . . .
Nobody Owes you Nothing

So you had a bad day:
You wanted sunshine, but were given rain
You expected joy, instead of pain
And when you laughed no one laughed with you . . .
Such a pain

Life seems unfair, and every time you try to express yourself no
one wants to go there . . .

Just remember they owe you Nothing

Sometimes we get tricked into believing we're all that
In our minds we are the and all in all
But no one else sees that

If you told them would they listen?
Hell, they barely pay attention.
Trying to get ahead by following he schemes of the dollar . . .
Marvin Gaye might shout,
"Makes me wanna holla!"
*Yet and still they do not owe you*

Who is accountable for your sin but the one who lives within?
Mama may have, Papa may have, but you are on your own
Your husband bought you a Benz,
You have a million friends,
And your funeral is paid before your death . . .
Still, nobody owes you Nothing

A dime, a dollar, a nickle, and a dime
You can complain and shout 'til your teeth
Fall out
This is not your day is what you tell
Every one from around the way . . .
WHO CARES???
No day is my day, yet I still do my thing
On my job no one know how creatively I flow
I am a nobody who knows somebody
Who knows everybody yet I am meaningless

Never mind what they say, I know that I exist

Don't let them hold you back because of what you lack
You are your only source of encouragement
On this place called earth

Now tell me, who owes you something?

R.S. White
4-20-01

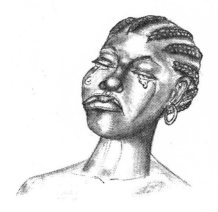

# What Happened to Your Spirit, Black Girl

Young girl, what happened to those sunny
Days which gave you a sunny gaze in your eyes

No longer do you laugh, you cry.

What happened to your gung
Ho, shake 'em down spirit.

Young girl

R.S. White
2/17/00

# *You Violated Me, You Stole from Me*

Creepin' dun crept into my space one too many times.
Creepin' dun crept and stole from me what was mine.
Creepin' dun crept and took all my goods away.
Creepin' dun crept and stole my life away.

Creepin' seeped through my door while I was esleepin'.
Took from me what creepin' should not have been seekin'.
Creepin' vi'lated me and stole me from myself.

Creepin' revisited me one summer noon.
Took all Mom's letters, thesis notes, and used shoes.
Creepin' crept and took my personals.
Creepin' knows me but I dun know creepin'.

Creepin' crept, stole, and violated me during times
when I was too blind to see
Creepin' crept and stole my life one childhood night; took from
me what was mine even before I knew what was right.

Creepin' dun came thru' one mo' 'gin one
Wednesday afternoon a week ago
Creepin' crept and stole my soul
Creepin' stole my tunes and blues away
Creepin' crept through da window and out da door.

Creepin' dun, dun me wrong one too many times
Stole my personals, my memories,
and da music which served as my sunshine.
Creepin' dun crept into my heart one too many times
Made me a woman, left me empty,
and opened doors locked with keys.

For some odd reason Creepin' keep on visiting me.

Roberta S. White
March 22, 2001
Inspired by the Break-In of my Jeep last Wednesday

# SEVEN: *The Number of Completion*

*I am not the man I used to be*
*One day God stepped in and delivered me*

## Stage One—The Lost Soul

**On Day One:** *God reached for my heart for God knew that by touching my heart I would have no choice but to hold His hand*
**On Day Two:** *God spoke to me and encouraged me to be fearless of this metamorphosis:*
*God shook me up, and put me down, He placed my feet on solid ground*

## Stage Two—Hunted By The Will Of God

**On Day Three:** *God convinced me that He is and I am not:*
*He took away my gifts, and talents, and possessions until I ran to Him begging for mercy*
**On Day Four:** *God removed people from my path, both good and bad, so that I solely relied on Him; In the beginning I felt lonely; good-bye pleasures of sin, no instant gratification, I thought I was broken*

*On Day Five: The Lord sat back in His rocking chair as he watched me search for ways to dodge Him; all along he had my coattail. I was running in circles, running, running, running*

## Stage Three-Submission To Divine Authority

*On Day Six: God sped up my race until I could run no more. I no longer desired worldly pleasures; I had a thirst for Christ. And I spoke these words, "Lord, I need a closer walk with thee. I need you to quench my thirst. I am lonely. Where are you God?*
*Where am I God? Why me Lord?*
*On Day Seven: God answered my questions when he began my Christian Journey as a pastor, a father, and a son of Christ. With God as my witness, I am complete!*

By Roberta Sonsaray White
Written June 6, 2002

**Dedicated to the**
*Rev. Dr. Joseph W. Daniels, Jr.*
*In celebration of 10 years of spiritual guidance*

# Kronos No More

Man, I clocked out about a year ago
Didn't know where I'd go, but knew I had to get out of the
Entrapment of man-made standards, expectations,
rules, and regulations
So I hit the clock

I hit it with my right fist
For with my left hand I was counting my hours
My hours equivocate my money:
*No money, no honey, no house, no car*
Shoot, I hit that clock with my left hand, too

Don't get me wrong,
I ain't claiming to be all I need to be
Nor am I professing to be rich
But I serve a God who is greater than the problems in my head
So I let go, and let God

In a dialogue with my Maker, He convinced me that
I could beat the odds
She God said that no work, means no eat,
But with faith and fate on my side
I'll be living sweet

My colleagues passed by as I stood
Front and center of Kronos
Some laughed, others joked
They thought my contemplation was an imitation
Of being "Hardcore" or a method of seeking attention
What they didn't know is that I was placed in this
Disposition
As frightening as it was for me to make the first move,
I knew my Father was waiting so I had to make it soon

Stereotypical slides of how my future would be served as the
numerals on the time clock
At *One*, I saw me lonely in a room, for it was already 12:30
which meant I'd be lonely soon
At *Two*, I saw myself crying out His name,
praising Him, and thanking Him all the same
At *Three*, I saw myself in misery wondering how could
God love me and let this be
At *Four*, I saw an open door and across from me
was a door that read, "Victory"
At *Five*, I became fearful of staying alive,
I felt like running to hide
But at *Six*, I had acquired enough strength
to gather my sticks of faith, courage, and wisdom
And place them by my side

At *Seven*, I walked through the door of limitation, stress, false
judgments, set backs, immorality, and personal attacks
At *Eight*, I was building a pass over from my sticks
and God taught me a few tricks
By *Twelve*, all was well, and God had shown me enough to
entrust me to move forward,
in this new life with no house, no telephone
All I had were the clothes on my back, a Bible, some faith, and a
desire to reach for a calling
As the slides began to transform back into numerals, my right
hand guided my time card through the machine
I clocked out & walked away
From my sad little dream

*In order to do what God called me to do*

Roberta Sonsaray White
8-31-02

# So Much Sorrow, So Much Pain

*I wonder when will I see the sun again?*
*How many times must one die before she lives?*
*How much must one give before he lives?*
*I ask these questions over and over again*
*And still I wonder, when will I see the sun again?*

*I used to smile and laugh at the moistness of the morning dew*
*I once enjoyed surviving my struggles and problems, too*
*Never once have I forgotten humankind*
*Yet still I am bewildered by life's wiles*
*And still I sing, when will I see the sun again?*

*No one ever told me the road would be so long*
*No one ever said that death was a safeguard from harm*
*No one ever said that laughter would erase the pain*
*All alone I wonder, when will I see the sun again?*

*Will there ever be a day when light shines on only me?*
*Is there a chance that I can have one year without misery?*
*Perhaps God would be so kind as to shine on only me.*
*But if not, then when will the sun smile on me?*

Roberta S. White
11-18-02

# Still Searching for the Promised Land

It came to me in a vision that this was not all God has in store
for my people

In this vision, I saw equality without colored or white faces; I
saw equality with no limitations

For the first time, I saw life as God planned it for me;

Speaking to me through the voices of people;
some my peers others not my equal

*We shall overcome*

Many moons and many days have passed
Yet and still, I wonder how much longer will this last

Days we've sat in scorn and defeat being cheated out of justice
that we seek

**Yet and still**
**How much longer 'til we overcome?**

Opportunities, they come our way sometimes we are not able to
receive them for one man made standard over another has us
torn between betraying our people or joining the leading class
*Yet and still when will all choices be equal?*

Somewhere I read or it was said that all humans
are created equal
If we are, why is race still a category on
College and job applications with "other" as
the discrete category label
*We are still in search of the Promised Land*

Could it be that God created this struggle for me?
Are we to suffer and let it be?
If it were so, God would have never instilled
the will to fight in me
*We shall overcome*

Roberta S. White
12-22-02

# *The Throne*

At the foot of my bed is where I am fed the word of life
The word of life cometh to me
from a spirit as sweet as the morning light

In this tranquil, bitter eve, I am able to receive a blessing
bestowed upon me by the Creator

It is at this foot that I am relieved of the weight of my sins and
totally forgiven again.

Oh yea sinner, gather 'round the foot of my
cushiony throne
With the spirit of Christ,
Let the Holy Spirit resonate in your ears

. . . And taste
Oh yes, taste and see that my God is a good God
One who feeds, and has bled so that He can lead us
to our destination

There is no friend like the lowly Jesus
No not one, not a single one
But thank You Redeemer for
comforting me in my time of need

Lord, I bow to You, again
Totally merciful, totally open to Your outcome
You have heard my praise even during my most trying days
Now all I need is a blessing from You

Step on in and shine, Lord God
Shine,
Not only for today, but for a lifetime
Let Your love pour on me
So that I may shine in the lives of others for You!

R.S. White
September 27, 2002

# The I[s] Have It

*Divided by the forces of the world:*
*Half of me desires things of man;*
*The other half of me longs to be what God is calling me to be.*
*I am a divided soul, how will thou rescue me?*

*I am a loving being full of pleasantries*
*I long to have a mate, I long to witness my fate,*
*Nevertheless, the I[s] have it and I do not receive favor.*

*I am a drum major for justice*
*Hear my percussion loud and clear*
*I am a god-fearing creature;*
*The Holy Spirit lives within*
*I am free as can be, no worries, no cares*
*The I[s] have it and I am what God wants me to be.*

*There is a warring in my soul between the worldly desires and*
  *righteous living*

*It's a diabolical schizophrenia that I do not understand*
*I have prayed to the Heavens, and waited for answers, yet still no sign*
*I know that my God is a good God who only blesses*
*Therefore, I will continue to prayer for the victory!*

Roberta Sonsaray White
10-25-02

# *Brotha*

Brotha wit' your pants sagging down,
Brotha don't you know you were born to wear a crown?
Brotha walking 'round not saying grace,
Brotha you can be gone and 'nother take your place.
Brotha you're one of a kind,
Brotha you refuse to unwind.
Brotha walkin' 'round wit' baggage on your heart,
Brotha dis old world gon' tear you apart.
Brotha carrying dat heavy load,
Brotha 'bout to EXPLODE!

Roberta Sonsaray White
April 3, 2003

In remembrance of Uncle Bobby

# *You Do Not Know Me*
# (But you know me very well)

I am the **child** standing on the
corner in the
morning
with nothing to do
No knowledge, no breakfast,
don't know my
parents
Love?
No thank you!
*See, you don't know me,*
*but you know me very well.*

I am the **young boy** who
dreams of being like Michael
Jordan, who aspires to earn
millions while crowds of
people surround me for
autographs.

*Encouragement?*
What is that?
My fourth grade teacher told
me I'd never amount to
nothing a long time ago.
Yeah, you don't know me, but
you know me very well.

I am the Little Miss, dark in
color who has
"The Bluest Eyes"
because the image of beauty is
Barbie:
slim, trim, and lighter than
myself.
If I keep wishing just maybe I
could be somebody else.
Black is beautiful?
Is it?

Well, a man once told me that
black is the color of sin
that with the color of my skin
I was condemned.
Do you know me now?
Of course you do.
You don't know me, but you
know me very well.

I am the **mother** with two,
three, four, five children who
believes that my husband is
somewhere around the corner.
Oh, you don't know that our
men are no good?
Well, that is what society tells.
Heck, all of my children don't
know their fathers.
You see me everyday, but you
still claim that you do not
know me.

I am the **black man** selling
whatever I can get in my
hands
I live, I love, and I dream

Because of the color of my skin
and the nature of my gender

People classify me as hopeless
even before they give me a
chance.

Bra, I'm just like you. I know
you see me everyday.
You don't know me? …
just another to turn and walk
away.

I am that **God-fearing individual**
filled with God's light
Sitting on top of bills and
challenges
*Don't know where my next meal
will come from.*
Yeah, I'm rich in faith, yet I
lack substance in my life.
Everyone knows me
I sit on the pew next to you
every Sunday.
I already know
"You don't know me, but you
know me very well."

You know me because I am the
reflection of you.
You know me because God
created both you and
I in His image
Yet you claim you have never
seen me.
Have you looked in the mirror
lately and seen your face
among the faces in your inner
city community?

47

Have you looked at your
colleagues, your church
members, or the very people
whose blood you share lately?

I am that lost **black child,**
That discouraged **black boy,**
That disillusioned **black girl,**
That insecure **black woman,**
That "hopeless" **black man,**
I am **your very neighbor** whose
hand you hold every
Sunday.

I am your reflection.
**Remember ME?**
—Roberta Sonsaray White
2-19-01

# *Misunderstood*

We are often misunderstood
Because we don't understand ourselves

We are often cast out
Because we fail to shout at appropriate times

Sometimes we are discouraged
Because no one took time to encourage us

Bottom line,
We must learn to do for ourselves

We often wonder how this will happen
When we have never had a model close at hand
How are we to be model citizens and future leaders
When it appears that no one gives a damn?

Is it possible for the blind to really lead the blind to a better way?
Or is it our responsibility to speak up and say:

This great nation in which we live has failed us
It has failed to teach us respect, love, and acceptance
This great nation, leading the world in technology advancements
Cannot even teach me how to maintain when my mother's at home
unconscious again

This great place we call "Land of the free, and home of the brave"
Has placed invisible chains around our feet; we are the new
born slave
This place where all men are created equal
Has revoked our right to choose whether we win or lose
By cutting financial aid to college
My grades were too poor in high school, there's no way I can win
a scholarship

We're just another link in the chain, the cycle,
of mental enslavement
If I had a choice, I would skip town and jump on a ship going
anywhere, Anywhere is better than here

I used to fear death, but no longer have I fear
Could it be, that I am living the worst of miseries?
This great nation has failed to teach my generation how to
succeed . . .
As a result, we shall forever bleed the pains of a dream deferred
We shall forever remain unheard.

Roberta Sonsaray White
11-18-03

# *Manic Friday*

Friday is a day most people look forward too
If you walked in my shoes, you'd dread Fridays, too
There's nothing to see
When you live a life of misery
Everyday of my life, I come home to an empty house
No dog, no cat, no maid, no spouse
Just silence . . . and a bird in my empty house.

So what makes Friday any different from Monday?
The weekend, a long, slew of consecutive days
When my alarm clock doesn't sound
No work to report too
No one to clown
Just me in silence . . . and a bird in my empty house.

I guess my Friday dread began about four years ago
When I received a call telling me Mama's going home
I stopped what I was doing
Couldn't believe what I'd heard
Instantly I dropped the phone

No mumbling, I screamed words,
Asked questions of how and why and what can I do
No one had an answer, no one knew
With fear in my heart, and the weight of a life time on my
shoulders
I never thought about what this would mean for Friday.

The weekend is not my friend
For I have no one to share it with
No one to love me, no one who cares
I'm tired of this lonely state of being
Some times I wish I were never born, never seen
And every week around this time
Friday rolls around
Just me in silence . . . and a bird in my empty house.

RSWhite
10-10-03

# DC: The Northern South

The northern, south that's what DC is
You can lose your life at the drop of a hat
Turn the corner and be greeted with a bat
Walk a block or two you meet people who act as if they know you:
Greeting you with southern waves,
extending hospitality and warmth
It'll make you wonder, "What's wrong with this joint?"
DC: The Northern South

Now if you tell these city folk they're southern to say the least
Some will challenge you
For they swear by claiming to be no. 1
or the crime capital of the nation
Then there are those who desire knowledge, and embrace values
while pursing a formal education
These folk don't mind fellowshipping
For in the south, this is what they do
And once again, it's like being on "Cheers"
because you feel as if everyone knows you
DC: The Northern South

Some might think it takes a lot of nerve to call DC the south
For out the mouths of many you hear
"The North is what it's all about"
Truth be told, DC is the median between the two worlds bold
Depending on whom you ask
The answer may sound absurd
Is DC the North or South?

Can you picture yourself buying a house in a city
where Blacks once reigned supreme;
A city where Blacks pursue the American dream?
Or do you view DC through present day eyes:
A city full of politics, run-down schools, and crooks whom lie?
A place where it's not safe to rest your feet; depending
On where you live, what you eat, and on whose block you meet
DC: The Northern South

No matter what you say, this debate can go on all day
Bring your thoughts to a close
And be grateful for the moments of peace
And
Street noise
DC: The Northern South

11-25-03

# *Pump My Fist*

Every morning I wake up:
Head on ache
Foot in pain
No financial gain
I pump my fist

Sometimes as I leave the unemployment line I . . .
Jump up and down and shout
Scream profanity at anyone listening to me
Realize ain't nothing changed
I pump my fist

There are times when I feel I have arrived:
Check in hand
Run to Footlocker for new shoes
Grab a bite to eat
Then head home broke
I pump my fist

When I think of my family I . . .
Cry for every goodbye that never came back
Feel depressed because dreams deferred
Can't hear Mama's loving words
Fail to see the God in us together
I pump my fist
I pump my fist
I pump my fist

Roberta Sonsaray White
11-25-03

# How Many Times

*So many times you could have lifted me up,*
*but instead you tore me down*
During moments when I didn't know where to go
you refused to show me how
*Every time I tried to express how much I need you*
Never once did you look me in the face
or listen to my words spoken
In this dense space.

Ever since the day mom went away, your love has been a closed door;
But when I become a statistic you plea,
"She had so much to fight for"
All my life I've been fighting,
Even up to the last stroke of this pen;
Depleted, deleted, defeated, in this race designed not to win.

What's the use in fighting if when won no one cheers?
It's a meaningless victory, abrupt to end.

Days I sit and wonder why God chose me to live
Everyday I live my life hoping that someone will love me
Before I leave here.

Mama's not here to push me along the way
God has intrusted my care to you; you reject me and go astray

I've been knocking at your door since I was knee high to a foot stole
Back then with Mama, you'd let me in
A parentless child is no less than a parented child.

Please listen to my words, to this small request:

This is a cry for help from the center of my aching Heart
straight to you
I thirst for your love as if it's something I've never known
Help me over the hurdles and walk me through the
Challenges
Pray me up a river
Whatever you do, do not leave me here

Roberta Sonsaray White
6-26-03

# *No Credit Needed*

A wise person once said, "A friend in need is a friend in deed"
For what is a person who does not have need,
But a lowly, disillusioned soul

Lord, You have blessed me with the finest and the best
So that I can share it with the world

I long to love, kiss, establish a relationship, grow, and grow old
with some godly man
But for now I am alone
Who can I call my own?

I need God's strength to carry on
I need God's might
I need God's grace to make it through
The night.

Amen

R. S. White
7-20-02

# *You Violated Me (Part 2)*

Creepin' dun crept back in again
Creepin' dun crept and stole my music, but that's not the end
Creepin' dun crept and stole my cash
Creepin's got my belongings, but Jesus got my soul
Creepin' needs to thank the Savior for blessing
me to maintain control
Creepin' don't know that no one can take what's God's
Creepin' don't realize that Jesus knows the odds: once bitten,
twice shy, the Creator is capable of transforming lives
Creepin' keep on comin' cause my heart is pure
Creepin' next time you come for me, I'll be even more secure
My Lord and Savior thanks for choosing me
Because Of Jesus, I am set free

Roberta Sonsaray White
April 14, 2003

# *Leaves On My Lot*

Who is liable for this mess I am in?
Who is responsible for my choosing to sin?
Who has been so bold as to tear down my guard?
Who has chosen to put leaves on my lot?

From the masses whom shall I blame?
For the choices I have made, my feelings of shame?
Is there anyone I can pinpoint such chaos to?
Who is to blame, when I am the only one who knew?
Who keeps putting leaves on my lot?

Just when I think I am freed up from sin
Temptation steps my way
And then I am dancing with Satan again
Afterward I feel so cold and lonely
It is at times like these I need God to hold me
Yet, I wonder why did I not desire God's touch when
The touch of man appeared to be so much
As I sit and think of the things I put myself through
I still question, who is strangling my lot with leaves, is it me or
is it you?

Who will take the blame for this here mess?
With whom can I approach my Maker and claim my innocence?
Am I the one to blame for my life's guilt and shame?
From whom did I learn such habits, are they to blame?
Tell me, who keeps putting these leaves on my lot?

Every time I collect a pile of leaves in different colors
I always find there is a leaf of another shade
Their shapes are many, too diverse to recall
All I know is their consequences affect us all
So how do they keep crossing my path?
Who is baring the leaves; they appear where there is no grass?

I marvel and contemplate with a mind full of stress
Knowing in my heart, if it were not for leaves
I would not be in such a mess . . .
Leaves on my lot

Roberta Sonsaray White
10-30-03

# REALIZATION

**1 Corinthians 13³**

¹²Now we see things imperfectly as in a poor mirror, but then we will see everything with perfect clarity. All that I know now is partial and incomplete, but then I will know everything completely, just as God knows me now.

Who are you? What is your purpose? Why did God place you in such a predicament? The answer: God created you to be great right now! Now that the struggle between self-gratification and Spiritual obedience has subsided, you have grown to a point where you desire more from life than temporary gratification; you want substance. Welcome to *Realization!* You have reached a point in your journey where you feel there is so much more to life than existing. All the lessons taught by the elders finally begin to make sense. You are able to reflect without pain. This is a good place to be, for it is at this stage you begin to witness and disciple folk unto God. You no longer fear alienation for God is all you need. The Creator is your everything and you are everything to the Creator. Finally, you are strong enough to speak from the heart.

Do not be dismayed for the journey to realization is not struggle free. Everyday we encounter messages, images, and people who try to convince us that who we are is not good enough. Far too often, we become victims of other people's ideas. We begin to question God, but not in the way we should. We want to know who we are. The truth is we already know the answer. The question we need to ask God is, "Who am I to You?"

In this section, you will be embraced by twenty-four selections that confront the question, "God, who am I to You?" As you actively read each piece, allow yourself to transform from the unknown to realization. Once you know whose and who you are it will be easier for you to respect yourself and others.

## Matthew 7[4]

[12] So whatever you wish that others would do to you, do also to them, for this is the Law and the Prophets.

# Mama used to say

Mama used to say . . .

If the good lord just hold us 'til next
Pay, I'll buy enough food to carry us
Along the way.
These are some words my mama
Said.

Girl, you can be anything you want to be,
Don't settle for a knucklehead,
Nor let anyone cause you misery.
My black queen, my mommy, said these words
To me.

I wish I were you and could say the things you do.
You are a good writer, Cakes;
Better writer than talker,
Lord knows you can talk!
Mama used to tell me my worth.

Mama wrote in a letter to me:
The world will be a better place because
You're in it.
Mama inspires me to move when I want to lie down.

Mama used to say,
Go Cakes!
"You got it going on"
We'd dance, laugh, and cry together

Lord, I miss my mama

Roberta S. White
In memory of my best friend,
My mother
5-26-02

# "ISMS"

*Racism is a shame*
*Sexism, another discriminating, incriminating name*
*Schemism sneaky devilish souls*
*Classism another word for control*
*Vandalism is destruction beyond belief*
*Thievism, the criminals who run our streets*
*Scandalism a way to bribe black leaders out of their position*
*Handalism, another word for leadership*
*Socialism means exclusiveness*

*The "isms" are a disease that nurture the upper class*

*The isms are spreading like*
*AIDS . . . how long will the poor last*

Roberta S. White
2/01

# R & B

The center of my soul is R & B
On days when I feel weary I sing the blues loud enough
for others to hear me
When my spirits are lifted I might play funk;
Mama always claims that, "Funk is junk."
If I X out loud & rowdy sounds that automatically means
that rock and roll can't stay around
I say no to reggae cause I can't move my hips
But give me some disco so I can move my lips
On days when I feel sassy sweet
I play some soothing jazz, lay back, rest my feet
Sometimes, that is every blue moon, I get the urge to dance a lot,
play hip-hop and groove
Oh, but everyday I breathe God's air
I play a melody of sweet Gospel music to brighten up my day.

R.S. White
3-9-02

# *Just as I am*

*Accept me as I am: without one single plea*
*Share with me your gentle touch, a prayer on bended knees*
*All my life I have prayed for someone like you*
*I've searched through many open doors, never to receive a clue*
*That my blessing on earth would come through you.*

*Sometimes we argue, fuss, and fight, but never will we*
*Close our eyes again without a hug, kiss, and the words "good night"*

*Challenges will come as they often do,*
*In each challenge I find comfort in knowing that I have you*
*You are my friend, you are my love,*
*You are God's gift to me here on earth.*

*Just as I am without a single plea*
*Others may not understand how our union came to be*
*Trusting in the God of creation opinions do not matter*
*Let's remain committed for life as friends and lovers*
*Just as we are*

■ Roberta S. White
■ 3-20-02

# Lest We Forget

Lest we forget we once occupied the seats
we some days glance at with scorn and defeat

These seats we, too, once occupied

Lest we forget at some appointed time
we feared the red ink of correction
And the screech of angry teacher chastisement

Ink and chastisement, too, once
Equaled failure

Lest we forget that somewhere in our subconscious mind
We, too, did something mean, evil, thoughtless, unkind

Cruelty and revenge at some time, too, was our secret friend

**Lest** we remember our call to bridge the
Gap in humanity's wall

*Lest we remember our past*
*in order to better understand*
*the challenges faced by our children*

*Lest we remember we are no longer*
*what we used to be, and with love, encouragement, and guidance*
*they, too, will some day be greater*
*than what they are today*

—Ms. Roberta S. White
3-26-02

# We Da Havenots

*By Roberta S. White*

*We da ones others ignore*
*We da ones society ties to destroy*
*We da ones who never hear 143 (I love you)*
*We da ones Gwendolyn mentions in "We Cool"*
*We da ones who have not lived,*
*No one ever gave us life*
*We Da Havenots*

*We da ones living in slums*
*We da ones smoking dope and drinking rum*
*We da ones without hope*
*We da ones unable to cope*
*We da ones others put down, don't want around*
*We Da Havenots*

*We da ones crowding corners*
*We da ones you fear want your daughters*
*We da ones having babies with no fathers*
*We da ones never make it to college*
*We da ones using double negatives, curse words,*
*and not afraid to live*
*We Da Havenots*

*We da ones society fear*
*We da ones always loud enough to hear*
*We da ones God chose to keep alive*
*We da ones excluded from elitism, suppressed,*
*And forgotten*
*We Da Havenots*

8-16-01

# *More Than Money*

*Created in the image of perfection*
*Men often view women as the object of their erection*
*"She wants the money" is what they chant,*
*failing to realize that all we want is romance*

*These hips, money did not buy*
*These lips, a physician's pension could not fit the cost*
*Creator God gave them all*

*Money is a necessity to pay the bills*
*However, peaking and maintaining a sista's interest requires a lot of skill*

*Speak to me in a tone of interest:*
*Ask about my past, my future, and my wishes*
*Look into my eyes as if you have never seen a more beautiful sight*
*Hold me in your arms as if tonight is our last night*

*Moments like these are priceless,*
*To be near cost you nothing, but love compassion, and empathy*

*When we met, I knew nothing about your wealth*
*All I wanted was your heart for me*

*My interest, your intentions*
*My concern, our future*
*My desire, to be your lady flower*

*So many times love passed me by because*
*I let men crawl between my thighs*
*Not this time*

*My mind's eye leads me to believe*
*That my game needs upgrading like*
*A Dell computer, so I will change*

*Still carrying more hips than a little bit,*
*The difference, no men will be kissing*
*Them with warm, moist lips*

*Do not misunderstand my plan, for I still want you to "Be my man"*
*I just cannot sell myself short by*
*distributing my Gucci for a broken heart*

*First, I will sell you my mind, so that I may*
*Purchase the key to your heart for me and only me*

*The amount of our currency exceeds dividends;*
*It requires us to be friends*

*In that vein, you are a millionaire for*
*You have me totally.*

R.S. White
8/11/01

# Here I am

*I remember when I was in the streets*
*And the streets were in me*
*I would hold on to the corner so tight*
*That I couldn't hear Jesus calling for me*

*Back then, I was doing my own thing consciously*
*While God was working through me subconsciously*
*I tried to shake the Creator because I wanted to continue on*
*The rugged path I trailed,*
*I really didn't want to continue,*
*But Satin convinced me that I'd never*
*Be able to return to my Savior*
*So I continued to walk in sin*

*On my journey to no where God sent His people to bring me home.*
*Mama prayed for me,*
*Daddy thanked God daily for my birth,*
*My siblings lifted me in conversation*
*And spoke into existence that someday soon*
*I'd return stronger, and more willing to serve the Lord,*

*As ironic as this may sound God sent me "street" people"*
*To convince me that I needed to reconnect*
*With my Savior*

*So I grew*
*Slowly with an unnoticeable effort*
*God reeled me back in*
*One morning when I was awaken by the purity of light*
*Shining on my day-old sinful body;*
*My new body in Christ,*
*I marched into the church to do what*
*I'd been called to do . . .*
*So here I am*

By Roberta S. White

# *Against The Grain*

*I never chose to be this way,*
*However, some how I am*
*I never understood how one could be condemned*
*For being what she never wanted to be*
*I have difficulty comprehending why many say I am going down*
*When then, like now, I seek You for my crown.*

*Lord, you know my faults*
*The many one by one I need not name*
*You know my heart,*
*Every prayer, every thought*

*In the sea of forgetfulness is where I lay my past*
*I ask that you will forgive my transgressions*
*And my transgressors*
*Even those whom I have failed to ask*

*A new day is dawning*
*My view is clearer*
*I see me as you have ordained me to be,*

*Walking forth from the dimming light*
*I see myself as you have created me,*
*Oh so pleasing in thy sight*

*Send forth your people who are for me*
*So that I never have to wonder*
*Lead me to places feared*
*Show me my strength bold and bright*
*Prepare a table for me in the presence*
*Of my enemies*
*Use me for your glory*

*And so it is*
*I am what God created me to be*

R.S. White
12-8-02
In dedication to Francine Andrews

# *Loc Prayer*

*'Til death do we part, I pray*
*Lord, keep my hair locked both night and day*
*Thicken my locs, that they may grow strong as cords*
*With spare strands sticking out*
*Lord, bless my locs to unite my strands of hair:*
*100,000,000 strong please help them to get along.*

*Lord, make my locs the epitome of beauty: radiant,*
*colorful, and orderly*
*Help them to be an example of the struggle of my people:*
*some short, others long, some weak, some strong, but*
*all-important and dependent on one another for survival*
*and*
*where one is weak, and another is strong, please allow them to*
*come together, intertwined for in Your word you said that where*
*ever two or three are gathered in Your name,*
*there too You will be*
*Lord, let them hold your love in each bunch: a faithful sign of*
*trust, no worries for their union is ordained by you.*

*And Lord, bless them to symbolize the hope of multicultural acceptance: different strands, various textures, intertwined into one loc and as many locs bless them to stand together in unity to represent the beautiful community of my hair.*

*Amen*

Roberta Sonsaray White
1-16-03, Edited 1-20-03

# Sundays Remind Me

*On Sunday, I am reminded that God is . . .*
*On Sunday, I am greeted by love in song and spirit*
*On Sunday, I am reminded that one sin yesterday*
*can be forgiven today*
*On Sunday, I hug and receive hugs from kindred spirits*
*On Sunday, I am reminded that my trials*
*and tribulations are stepping stones: weight*
*training for the blessings to come*
*Sunday reminds me of Grandma's collard greens,*
*fried chicken, and grape kool aid*
*Sunday reminds me of Mama's Bible reading,*
*encouragement, conversations about love, hugs and kisses*
*Sunday reminds me of confrontations with my sister:*
*hitting, kicking, and screaming;*
*followed by hugs, kisses, laughs and love*
*Sunday reminds me of family gatherings,*
*large hats, gospel hymns, and friends.*

*Lord, I wish every day were Sunday.*

Roberta Sonsaray White
10-20-02

# *Testimony*

*I come to you, my friend (love, mom, dad, etc.)*
*Not to ridicule you in anyway,*
*But to deliver a testimony here today.*

*Now when I was dead in sin*
*It was the God of Creation who took me in.*

*I, too, was doing the things the unsaved do,*
*But God . . .*
*God thought enough of me to lend*
*Me a single plea of forgiveness and grace.*

*I found this odd because I've never seen His face.*
*Or is He a She made masculine by me?*
*Nevertheless, my God is the leader of my*
*night and day-always by my side making a way.*

*Let me see if I can make this thing clearer,*
*If I can help you see what*
*God has done for me.*
*I spent many nights in ungodly arms, now*
*I realize Jesus kept me safe from harm.*
*Many days I stressed life's mess*
*Only to learn that in His bosom*
*I could find rest.*
*I have blessed and cursed out of these lips*
*But God . . .*
*God helped me to get a grip on my tongue*
*By turning my anger into praise*
*Oh, if you could have seen me then,*
*today you'd be AMAZED!*

*Praise God for deliverance!*

*Now I say all of this to help you understand*
*That by choosing God's way does not*
*Threaten your credibility as a child, parent, woman, or man.*
*For the Creator wants what is best for you.*
*Know that no matter where you are, only God can deliver you.*
*Go in PEACE*

By Roberta S. White

# *The Seasons*

*Summer loses her leaves to fall*
*Fall turns the bright green leaves to beautiful yellow, orange, brown,*
*and green leaves*
*Winter comes and gives the leaves rest*
*Spring steps in and gives the leaves breath*
*Then summer rolls around again to give the leaves life!*

Roberta Sonsaray White
Dedicated to Mr. K.J. Neat and Pre-K

# *Books*

The greatest gift one could ever give is a **book** . . .
Filled with **knowledge**
With the **knowledge** that carries one through school
And maybe . . . through **college**
Perhaps the child may go beyond **college** education
**This child may someday run the nation!**

If this child runs the **nation**
Oh, what **a glorious country** this would be
For at a young age this child received a **book**
The **book** taught concepts in prose and rhyme
It taught the child that though **Black,**
He could **climb**
Beyond the tops of **corporate ladders**
Onto achieving something as great as

**Preaching a Sermon on the Mount**
**Or**

**Leading a discussion** on war relations
On each page fresh ideas are **discovered**
And a young girl **learns** that she
Can be greater than **Halle Berry**

*Or*
*She can explore without gravity limitations*
*like **Mae Jemison** in space*
*For the first time in her life*
*This young girl realizes that **in this***
***World she has a place***

*In a **gift book** a child can see*
*That **schools neglect to** teach accurate history*
*They learn that **on the backs of others** this great nation stands*
*However, they are taught that much is the ingenious*
*Of the White man*
*They learn that **King and Parks** ushered the struggle for civil rights*
*However, what they fail to learn*
*Is that **others were instrumental in the plight***

***Great journeys await** your child inside the cover of a book*
***Don't take my word for it,***
***Open a book and take a look***
*Go ahead; send your child off to great lands to **explore***
*In a book, **your child does not have to remain the same***

*For goodness sake, **give them a Bible FIRST!***
***Teach** your children of **God's GREAT WORTH***
***Lead** them to examples of falter and success*
***Teach** the children that they, too, can be the VERY BEST*
***Shop** in Karibu, Barnes & Noble, and Books A Million, too*
***Increase** their exposure by reading to them, too*
*And **in exchange** for a great mechanical game*

***Give them knowledge tangible and true***
***Present** them with a book*
*So that they can **learn of life's truths***

87

*Give every child the gift of a book*
*Knowledge is indispensable*
*Don't take my word for it,*
*Open a book and take a look*
*See for yourself the great mysteries that*
*Lay inside of a BOOK!*

Roberta Sonsaray White
3-1-03

# *Wisdom*

*This one is for the person who heeded Mom's advice:*
*Before you marry, my child pray thrice*

*This one is for the individual who listened to the word preached:*
*There shall be no other gods before Thee*
*and*
*you shall love your neighbor*
*as yourself!*

*This one is for the one who became humble in times of challenge:*
*You held your tongue and God granted you grace*

*This one is for the one who absorbed Papaw's foresight:*
*God is capable of making something out of nothing: look at all God*
*has done for you!*

*This one is for the one who cared enough to listen to a child:*
*I know I can be what I want to be.*
*And guess what?*
*You can TOO!*

*WISDOM*

Roberta S. White
4-17-03
(Dulles International Airport)

# This One Thing (Is True)

*Let there never come a day*
*That I open my eyes and you are not near*
*Everyday let your words comfort my ear*
*If ever a tear should fall,*
*Let it be your name I call*
*I have loved and not loved before,*
*But this one thing is true*
*I am gratefully in love because of you*

*We vowed to keep our feelings few, far, and in between*
*We agreed to remain detached*
*Yet we continue to share many special things*
*Two lonely souls roaming in a world so free*
*Let's put away our shields*
*So that this love-thing can be*
*This one thing (is true) you are love to me and I am love to you*

*No more searching need I do*
*For in you I have discovered love anew*
*No other man can capture my attention*
*For in your hand my heart expands*
*No more wondering if I can love again*
*Faith in God has erased all our sins*
*This one thing (is true) if ever there was love, Baby I found it in you*

*This one thing (is true), you are the love I never knew*

Roberta Sonsaray White
8-13-03

# First Time

*For the First Time in my life,*
*I'm going to live it right*
*I refuse to let my light shed*
*On that ugly enemy's head*
*For the First Time in my life, I'm going to live for God*

*So many times before*
*I said I lived for God but ignored*
*The plagues birthed into this world by he*
*Who was cast out of Heaven*
*And confined to a life of misery*
*If I ever repented before*
*Just to turn and submit to my own will*
*I surrender my life unto*
*My Lord, and Savior still*
*I surrender all to the One who never left me*
*Who never forgets me*
*And loves me ever still*
*For the First Time in my life I'm going to live it right*

*Temptation tries to haunt me yet*
*Especially when I'm at God's best*
*She tries to sink her teeth in me*
*To make my life feel like misery*
*He always finds me when I'm alone*
*Resting in my nice, clean home*
*Or maybe I've just finished praying to God*
*It seems like after "Amen" Satin shows*
*Up in odd places*
*Where there are people I know*
*When I look into their eyes*

*And think that I know who they are*
*The spirit steps in and discerns that in this moment*
*They are not so*
*Then I'm left feeling such a mess*
*I wonder why so much temptation, why so much stress*
*Has God forgotten me amidst all life's bliss*
*Then I reflect on the Devil's word, "Stress"*
*I realize, God is not the author of confusion*
*Nor does God usher the evil thereof*
*Although I must fight the temptation*
*I know God loves me enough to equip me with tools*
*Powerful enough to be receptive of GRACE*
*I now know, Satin has no place with the righteous For the First Time*
*in my life,*
*I'm going to live it right*

*I know this may sound crazy, and almost impossible to understand*
*But before I even knew me*
*My God already had a plan*
*For the details of my life*
*From day to day*

*When I contemplate on the Word*
*I realize I was designed to stay and*
*Stand on God's Word*
*No, I do not look like the American Dream or*
*A European Queen*
*But deep in my heart I believe that I can have all that is of God*
*While my road may be rougher than the average*
*Adult my age*
*I find comfort in knowing that I have strength that's amazing*
*For the First Time in my life,*
*I'm going to live it right*

*I'm holding on to God's promises of peace,*
*Favor, and refuge*
*I'm reminding God that God chose me and*
*Of God's plans for good*
*I'm petitioning Jesus to take my request*
*To God*
*I'm relying on my faith to give me peace with every stride*
*I'm calling on Saints to carry me with them in prayer*
*For I know my prayers, coupled with those of the righteous*
*Are sure to get me to the feet of the Most High*
*For the First Time in my life,*
*I'm going to live it right*
*For the First Time in my life,*
*I'm going to live it right*
*With conviction, humbleness, mercy, and faith I say with strength*
*For the First Time in my life,*
*I'm going to live it right*
*For the First Time in my life, I'm going to live for God*

Roberta Sonsaray White
10-18-03

# Spiritual Break Through

*It came at a time when I didn't see it coming:*
*Like a thief in the night, it knocked on my door*
*Filled with the darkness of death and*
*illuminated by the light of a blessing*
*It remained latent, and patiently waited*

*She spoke to me:*
*Said something about she'd always been with me*
*Wanted to kiss me*
*And see me at my best*
*She said I ignored her, feared her, yet desired her all the same*

*He said*
*I was created for him and he for me*
*Then he looked at me with eyes of love and*
*told me all that I could be*
*He said for so long he waited for this moment to touch my hand*
*He would have tried sooner, but feared I wouldn't understand*
*So he waited until today*

*It went on to say that now is an opportune time*
*To seek abundance:*
*In an economy suffering from Wall Street's failure, the Middle Class*
*being the lower class because of their refusal to denounce power*
*within their reach*
*She/He went on preaching to me*
*He painted his point of divine timing, spiritual alignment, and*
*purpose oh, so clear*
*With the way she spoke I soon had no fears*
*All I could see were the endless possibilities;*
*I saw myself being as great as I wanted to be*

*Just as smooth and shocking as he came in*
*He walked out the door*
*Not another word did I hear*
*Until I walked through God's door*
*Just as I swung the door handle free*
*There before my very eyes was my life's purpose waiting for me.*

Roberta Sonsaray White
11-6-03

# A Time Like This

*I bet you wondered why God*
*denied you that new position*
*I bet you wondered why*
*sometimes your children chose not*
*to listen*
*From time to time, you may have*
*wondered why your loved ones*
*have forsaken you*
*Why, why, you ask?*

*Sometimes I have wondered why*
*God made me homeless,*
*parentless, and creative*
*I've asked God why have my kin*
*chose gin & sin over righteousness*
*I have even had to question my*
*sinful choices*
*Why, why, I ask?*

*As each day unfolds in life, I*
*better understand*

*That these trials and tribulations*
*you and I face*
*Are designed to help us help*
*someone else*
*Run this race*
*My suffering is your gain*
*And your pain, is my gain*
*Our joys are multiplied when we*
*can stand side by side*
*Hand in hand, lifting one*
*another toward the Master's*
*Plan*

*It took me a while to see*
*That God chose me to receive the*
*victory*
*It took me some time to know*
*That only from struggle can the*
*strong truly grow*
*Daily I learn*

*That each is called to a plan,*
*prepared, and pruned*
*To stand where the uncalled*
*might fall*
*God equips us and when we*
*surrender our own will*

*Our reward is to give, so others*
*may live.*

*Yes, you were created for this*
*moment in time*
*A time when people are*
*struggling to smile, women are*
*hopelessly hopeful, and men are*
*at the end of their rope*
*Yes, you were created for a time*
*like this*

*A time when children are rushed*
*to be adults, and respect is a*
*word, the actions are not taught*
*Yes, your struggles were designed*
*to strengthen you*
*Someone needs you right now*
*I need you right now*
*Someone needs me*
*You need me right now*
*Like you, I too, want to be all*
*God calls me to be*
*For there is no place, I would*
*rather be than in God's will*
*We were created for a time like*
*this*

Roberta S. White
11-23-03

# *Made it Yet?*

*Some of us ain't made it yet:*
*We still round here trying to figure out*
*Jesus' name*
*Looking at bills, no means to pay*
*Frustrated by lack of concern*
*For the people in the hood who keep getting burned*
*Black skin, white skin, Hispanic/Asians, too*
*Treated unkindly as if*
*2/3s of a human we due*
*We just like you, we want to live*
*No one cares, no one gives*
*We ain't made it, we ain't made it*

*Ask yourself, "What does it mean to make it?"*
*It can't be a house, two kids and a pet*
*Many with these things receive a monthly check*
*Check one, check two*
*Count your pennies wisely or else you're through*
*Until next payday*
*We ain't made it yet*

*How will we know when we made it?*
*Will there be harps in the street,*
*People singing*
*And passing out TVs?*
*What does making it smell like?*
*Will there be sausages hanging from a vine*
*Will there be mangos made into wine*
*Will children be free to run in the streets?*
*What will the cops say when we're sitting on their home leather seats?*

*When will we make It*
*How long before long is long gone?*

Roberta Sonsaray White
11-25-03

# *Around The Corner*

*Take a look*
*The answer is not in a book*
*You never know what lurks around the corner*

*Many fear what may be*
*Too blinded by what they can see*
*You never know what lurks around the corner*

*Could it be your fate?*
*Perhaps it is your mate*
*Maybe it is a job long over due*
*Which you never knew was right for you*
*You never know what lurks around the corner*

*Isn't life a game of chance*
*You dance, kiss, court, and romance*
*Invest your time in what appears to be true*
*All because it feels good to you*
*You never know what lurks around the corner*

*One more mile to go*
*If you stop here you might miss your show*
*Too afraid of letting your past go*
*Because there's one who hurt you*
*Oh, so deeply*
*You keep holding on*
*To that sad song*
*He/She did me wrong*
*But you never know what lurks around the corner*

*What if you didn't have to look that far*
*What if your blessing was standing right where you are*
*Would you know what to do with it*
*Or*
*Would you leave it standing lonely because of fear*
*You never know what lurks in your face*

*Take a chance*
*Go on a date*
*Dial 411 instead of 911*
*Trust and believe*
*That what you desire is in your face or around the corner.*

Roberta Sonsaray White
9-16-03

# Oxymorons

Ain't a dang thang funny bout what is bout to be said
Just seems like for women, things are always this way
In society we are often classified as weak
Yet soon as a man ends up in trouble it's our help, our strength he seeks

When we are lonely with no mate we are classified as gay,
Soon as a man gets dissed he chooses to
Roll the same way
But we're gay?

It just ain't fair how we are overlooked for promotions
But as soon as a job goes bad
It's our skill the man wants us to devote to 'em.

Is it possible for God to call a woman into the ministry?
If so it is hard to tell when over 90% of all churches
Refuse to allow called women to excel.
Oh, it's cool for a woman to perform secretarial duties
Arrange activities for the children

*And usher folk to their seats*
*But when it comes time to receive the word of God*
*It's their presence, God's word you will not see.*
*Have you ever heard pastor say, "Girl you got a powerful testimony"*
*but refuses to allow her test to cease moans?*

*This thing is confusing*
*So much women have to give*
*But it's that one selfish creature that refuses to let the world see her live*
*It ain't that we are unstable creatures or we need to be affirmed*
*We affirm the masses, and in return, we get burned!*

Roberta Sonsaray White
6-29-03

# In the way of Goodness

*Move, move, move*
*Step aside*
*I've got a new attitude; got a new guide*

*Time came ticking down my block*
*Never thought anyone could rock my spot . . .*
*They can't cause what I have is for me*

*Years have passed, seasons long gone*
*For so long I sang the same song,*
*"somebody done me wrong"*
*All along I was the somebody I referred to in my song*

*Somebody told somebody, and some one told me*
*All the things I would never, could not be*
*I listened and believed*
*Then began to tell myself I couldn't achieve*
*And so I didn't*

*Move, out of my way*
*Many call on satan to get thee behind*
*Have you ever wondered whether or not*
*It was you who needed to get behind*
*Images are only as good as the thinker*
*So is it you or satan that supresses the plans of your maker*

*Go on and move, move something*
*Mystical said it best,*
*"shake it fast, watch yourself" now show you what you're working*
*with you'd be amazed how only beauty can come from the*
*descendants of slaves*
*shake it, shake it, shake it for the road, shake it again*
*Shake off the defeat*
*Tell yourself you're gonna win*

*And tell the negative thee to get behind the positive me!*

Roberta Sonsaray White
10-30-03

# Lessons

Some things I had to learn along this road of life
If I choose to live for God, things just might go right
In the end all things happen according to plan
But the consequences are greater when you live according to man

Every shut eye ain't closed and every "Good bye" ain't gone
These are two lessons I carry along
Just when you think he's out of your life for good
He comes back with a mere apology
And things appear to be like they should
Often times we know in our hearts
We're in a no good situation
But Sista so and so said, "Pray for him.
God will provide reservation."
So you do
But the truth still remains that a man who
loves you would not abuse you
In the word it says:
Love is patient, love is kind
What does the word say about someone who's
Working hard to make you lose your mind?

*Yes, in the Word it speaks of long suffering,*
*But how long must you suffer as if there is no ending?*
*These questions I pose to you*

*Sometimes in this life it is the woman who must stand and say,*
*"I'm leaving you."*
*God is able to provide your needs*
*Do not compromise yourself, do not lose your self esteem*

*There are so many lessons to be learned, so little time*
*Save yourself the heartache*
*Learn from what was mine*
*I've been hurt a time or two*
*It took a lot of prayer and encouragement for me to*
*Leave, too*
*But once I did, my burdens were less*
*Need I mention it took away my stress*
*What a joy peace brings*
*What a blessing release sustains*

*Keep one eye open for the good bye that ain't gone*
*Keep both hands clasped, God hears your song*
*Trust, Act, and Move on*

Roberta Sonsaray White
9-29-03
Written for female domestic abuse victims

# RESPECT

## Matthew 7[5]

[6] Do not give what is holy to the dogs; nor cast your pearls before swine, lest they trample them under their feet, and turn and tear you in pieces.

*Respect*, what does this word mean to you? Is respect something others give to us? Why is it important? The answers to the fore mentioned questions depend on what you have gathered so far along the spiritual journey. We have survived the stage of *conflicts* where there is a war between Spirit and flesh. By the end of this stage, we grow to realize that God wants what is best for us. We understand that in each conflict, we grow closer to our Creator. This leads us to a point of *realization*. At this point, we begin to accept the reality that there is more to life than bills, sex, pleasing others and ourselves. It becomes clearer to us that all we have endured will help us to serve God in the manner in which we have been called. It is when we understand whose and who we are that we can respect ourselves and others thus demanding respect in return.

Welcome to *respect!* This is a profound point in your walk with Christ. The Word constantly reminds us to care for our temple which is our Spirit in the flesh. When we understand all that God has invested in us, it is only right that we honor the Redeemer by caring for all that God leads us to. Respect is not just a word; it is an act, an attitude, and a way of life. Respect is acknowledging the fact that you are the best. Respect is believing in others even when people have given up on you. Respect is giving your all to everything because you know that Christ gives his all. Respect is who we are, what we are, and all that we hope to be in the name of Jesus Christ our Lord and Savior.

In this section, you will witness fourteen examples of respect at its best. You will savor the flavor of giving, receiving, and embracing others and self. Remember that loving self is wholesome, not arrogant. It is respectful when done with grace and humility. God wants us to acknowledge our greatness in the Spirit. You are great! Go on and testify!

## I Corinthians 4[6]

[3] I care very little if I am judged by you or by any human court;
indeed, I do not even judge myself.

# Acknowledge Me

*I am the princess of darkness:*
*An Eagle in the sky;*
*I am a queen with locs:*
*Brown tipped & dyed*
*I am an unseen leader in the eyes of others*
*All I ask is that you acknowledge me*

*Give me your assets*
*And I will make them grow*
*Tell me your expectations, I will tell you what I know*
*Look me in the eyes when my lips part like the Red Sea*
*If you plan to Honor God*
*You must acknowledge me*

*How can you scream "United We Stand" when you cast me down*
*Where is the togetherness when you refuse to see my face in the crowd*
*Why is it that you credit the ingenuity of the light*
*When it is the wisdom of the colored*
*That brought forth the knowledge pleasing to thy sight*
*Even if you choose to not see me, all I ask is that you acknowledge me*

R.S. White
3-9-02

# DON'T FORGET ABOUT BLACK

## DON'T FORGET ABOUT BLACK

Ye hear
When you've made it to the top
Making millions and selling a lot

## DON'T FORGET ABOUT BLACK

Ye hear
When you're face appears on
People magazine
And Essence tries to call you
Only to discover that your phone
No longer rings

## DON'T FORGET ABOUT BLACK

Ye hear
Cause y'ain't got to work
A 9-5
Some folk still in da hood
Tryin' to stay alive

## DON'T FORGET ABOUT BLACK

Ye hear
When lil'Betsy Jane loves ya last
year's draws
And she fillin' ya up with sweet
nothin's
Just to leave you
And take it all

## DON'T FORGET ABOUT BLACK

Ye hear
When ya sittin' next to denzel on a
Movie shoot
Sippin' on scotch, settin' on the rocks

## DON'T FORGET ABOUT BLACK

Ye hear
When dem folk turn dey backs
On ye and dem der you thwat
You knew
No longer want you

# DON'T FORGET ABOUT BLACK

*Ye hear*
*When we marching for a cause*
*Cuz ya people still ain't free*
*And even on Sundays we*
*Fail to touch and agree*
*Too scared somebody gone get*
*ahead*
*Rather see 'em dead than ahead*

# DON'T FORGET ABOUT BLACK

*Ye hear*

*even when you don't need us,*
*come on 'round*
*Ye hear*

# CAUSE WHEN YE REMEMBER BLACK WE ALWAYS GOT YA BACK

Roberta S. White
7-12-02

# I Deserve

I listened to what someone told
me yesterday about myself
And ended up where I stand
today
Standing in this present place, I
turn my head to
Review scenes from my past
From where I stand, I have a
record of accomplishments
Therefore, why did I believe her
when she said that I would not
make it
On what I have,
When she said that I needed to
start from the basics
To do what God has called me to
do?
I was vulnerable, and almost
Allowed someone, from
somewhere

To discourage me from achieving
my adolescent dream.

Today I realize that it is out with
the old and in with the new
I am on my way to walking on
through
God will send me what I need in
order to succeed
I will be strengthen to move
mountains
For I have faith the size of a
mustard seed
I am destined to be great
By choice and
By ordination
I must move beyond these walls
of 1820
Into a world of possibilities
Given by God

*I must tell my story, herstory, and*
*the stories of my people*
*I must represent the under*
*represented*
*Speak for the unspoken*
*Teach to the unteachable*
*Moreover, love the unlovable*
*In short, I must do what God*
*has told me will*
*Bring peace to my soul*

*The more I think about*
*yesterday,*
*The more I realize that it was*
*not all that bad*
*Had it not been for yesterday,*
*I would not have made*
*it to the blessings*
*Of today*

*With fatih I march forward with*
*hopes and dreams*
*Knowing full well that I deserve*
*God's*
*Highest honor*

*As a child of the King and*
*Queen of Creation*
*I am grateful for the poetry I will*
*write,*
*The lives that will be saved,*
*In addition, the achievement of*
*my dreams.*

**Roberta Sonsaray White**
**July 6, 2002**

# My Song

*Mama used to say I couldn't hold a tune*
*Well, no one holds a B-flat like me*

*My B-stands for blues and lack*
*Oh, maybe I can't hold a tune,*
*But I sure can sing the blues*

*B, bad girl blues, win some days,*
*Most days lose*
*Give and take such a sad mistake*
*So I cry and lie to pass the time of sadness*
*Yeah, it's the B-girl bad B, girl blues*

*If mama could see me now with no desire for school*
*what would she think?*
*If I told her that I want to sing, what would she think?*

*Mama, I want to sing my blues across the nation*
*One B-flat note at a time*

*I, I, I, want to tell of my past and the way you loved me*
*My whole life*

*Yeah, the B, bad girl blues . . .*
*I'll sing, dance, cry, but I refuse to romance 'til God*
*Sends 'em with a ring*
*For my tiny hand*
*Mama, I'm awaiting on my husband-man*
*Oww! Ow! It's the B-girl, bad girl, B-bop blues*

*No more song I sing but dis' one little 'ting*
*Me don't want no trouble, just love, shelter, and a ring*
*ME don't want no part-time lover or friends who skat*
*Like fleas*
*Me just want some B, bad girl lovin'*
*Me just want to sing . . . Yeah!*

By Roberta S. White
4-2-01

# Why We Can't Give Up
# On Black Men

*We, the inclusive form of "I" can not turn our backs*
*On the men who have been dealt a bad hand*

*This here is not a petition or call for sympathy;*
*Rather it's enlightenment, reality*

*We were born from the juices of an Ebony Creature*
*Our minds, body, and soul are reflections*
*Of this empowered thinker yet we've forgotten our place in the race of*
*survival*

*We need not think a promotion to CEO separates us from*
*The classification of our race; for both the educated and un,*
*Black/dark as Cain are forbidden to the lighter image*

*Our men need our patient spirit to love, nurture, and support;*
*They need our hands in marriage in order to produce*
*More of our own; our men need to hear the words "love", faith, and*
*success at the very least they need to be reminded*
*of unachievable peace*

*We can and will because we are*
*The beginning of Creation;*
*The first descendants of civilization*

*Sisters, hold on to your chocolate king for we*
*Know that milk and chocolate make cream, but*
*Chocolate and chocolate produce the*
*American Dream*

R.S. White
4/21/01

# Dependence

*All hell to the woman who denies herself*
*Piece of mind, fame and wealth*
*To walk behind a male of*
*Lesser value than herself*

*All prayers for the ladies who ignore their conscience*
*To be the "other" to someone else*
*Who does not respect their unique attributes*

*Dependent Sister, I hope you are listening,*
*For these words are for you . . .*

*The you who refuses a natural for the sake of permanent dependency on*
*Chemical treatment*

*The you who depends on a man for physical treatment,*
*completion,*
*and*
*stimulation of body,*
*Not soul*

*The you who belittles yourself, and believes you need him to make you whole*

*Dependent Sister,*
*Let that no good man go*

Roberta Sonsaray White
8-9-02

# Reclaiming

This thing here is a reclamation of the woman I gave up to
become what society wants me to be
I gave up my weight, my sanity to chase after a me that could
never be
I have starved myself to the point of no return
Only to learn that what I have is what I have earned
I do not suit a model's size, nor will you see me in Vogue because
My thighs are larger than the average size
But that's just fine because I accept me

I have wanted to be accepted, only to end up rejected
I tried to be, all along refusing to see what my God has for me
I have reached for the prizes of others' only to learn
That if I do not rejoice in what I have, God will never allow me
to earn
My just reward for being true
To the me God calls me to be

I am a Full-Figured Queen,
Look at my body, and my hips
I am full of life, love, and living
Not concerned with wealth
For I am rich in the acceptance of myself

I love me,
Every crease in my flesh,
I love me,
Every wrinkle, every depth
I love me,
Every mark that bares my strength
I love me.
Every challenge that I bequeath (face)

I am strong in this here figure that I sport
I am righteous in that I refuse to sell myself-short on someone
else's definition of beauty
For if I were not beautiful God would never have created me

*I am a Full-Figured Queen*

Roberta Sonsaray White
8-9-02

# *Righteous Sista*

It's something about my BlackBrotha,
But what about my Righteous Black Sista?

What about that lady who is oh, so, fly

You know, the one who holds a job, takes care of the house, yet
and still does not have a spouse.

## That Righteous Black Sista?

It's something about my BlackBrothas, I love ya,
But what about showing some love for my Righteous Black
Sistas?

What about the sista who loves her people, and even when
discriminated against, she loves others as equals?

You know, the one who is confronted with racisim everyday on her
job, yet and still she does not harbor a bad bone in her body?

# That Righteous Black Sista?

It's something about my BlackBrotha, I love ya,
there is no one above ya,
But what about the sista whom no one ever glorifies?

What about the sista who has paved the way for you and I, the
sista whose efforts were scorned as a diabolic cry?

You know, the sistas like Harriet Tubman, Phyllis Wheatley,
Marian Wright-Edelman, Oprah Winfrey, the Delaney Sisters,
Maya Angelou, Gwendolyn Brooks, and the list goes on . . . and
on . . . and on . . . ?

# Those Righteous Black Sistas?

It's something about my BlackBrotha, I love ya, there is no one
above ya, I want you to know that I'm here for you forever true,
But what about the sista who has no one to call on?

What about the sista who calls her brotha true and he calls her a fool?

You know, the kind of woman who will die for her man; sin sick
in love for her brotha of dark kin; overwhelmed and over worked,
and oh, so unappreciated?

# Those Faithful, Righteous Black Sistas?

Roberta Sonsaray White
7-28-02

# *A Dedication*

*I don't know what my God has for me,*
*But I know it must be great*
*So many times I could have died,*
*But He has kept my fate.*
*My destiny I do not know,*
*But trust that God will reveal my purpose for being tried and true,*
*For shedding a tear which is a sign . . .*
*I love you*

*Why did I have to meet you and never see your face?*
*I heard you moan, with little groans of ailing aching pain*
*As I pulled near I heard a scream that sent me into left field*
*Had I not heard the voice*
*I would have had no other choice than to take us out of here.*

*I thank God for being a keeper,*
*And keeping us near the cross*
*I thank the Lord for loving us, and saving you*
*From a loss*

*If we ever meet again*
*I hope it's on better terms*
*But 'til we meet face to face,*
*My prayers, my friend, you have earned.*

Roberta Sonsaray White
9-23-02
**inspired by a motorcycle accident in Forrestville, MD**

# I Don't Mind Being Black

Some things in this life I mind,
But being Black is not one of them

Some days I have withstood attack
Because my skin is Black,

**But I don't mind**

I have witnessed racial profiling
At its best
I have seen my sisters scorned
For wearing naturals flowing
Like the Red Sea
I have touched the hands of men
Tall as trees, dark as night
Hmm, **I don't mind being Black**

If I had a choice of colors,
You know which one I would choose
One thing I can say
Is that when you choose Black,
You can't lose

*Yeah, Black people have fallen short*
A time or two
But I keep things in perspective
By understanding the called are few
Still, **I don't mind being Black**


Considering all my people fought for
You know that **Crispus Attucks** was colored,
And first to be gunned down in the war

You know **Matthew Henson** crossed the Russian seas,
Heck he aimed high to explore
In 1909 he became the first man of color to walk the North Pole
Now you know that no one wanted to give credit
To this "Colored Boy"

**Bessie Coleman** had dreams of soaring high
**Sister** climbed in a plane
And headed straight for the sky
**Zora Neale Hurston** saw that men could do it too
So she put a pen to paper and
Told us what she knew
**Langston Hughes** had a song
To sing
He posed the question

*"What Happens to a dream?"*
Then Dr. **King**

showed us what happens

When a dream occurs

Now with this legacy of leaders,
*I don't mind being Black*

If I must stand armed
With a sword in my hand
I will
For I have come too far to be condemned (killed)

**I don't mind being Black**

Roberta Sonsaray White
2-23-03

# *Not By the Wayside*

I refuse to let another go
To watch the wind take another blow
I will not allow myself
To see my sister fall to her death
**I will not** in this very breath

**Lose another sister by the wayside**

I often wonder how they made it over
They being **Harriet Tubman, Sojourner Truth, and
Madame CJ Walker** to name a few

**How did they make it on so much less**

How did my sisters rise to
Be the very best
How did they do it on little or nothing at all
How did they stay abreast
Without taking a fall

How did these sisters make a way for both
You and I here today?
How did they do it
I do not know
How did they do it?
**What did they sow?**

My grandmother once said
At the end of community is
The word unity
Unity is the word that unites us in vocabulary
But what will keep us together
When the adversary comes to tear us apart?

**Who is capable, among us, to keep us from falling?**
We are

My sister, you are my keeper and I am here for you
Truer than life itself, I will see you through
I know that I have fallen short in my day
I ask that you will forgive me,
That you will allow me to usher you along the way
*You are my reflection*
Every struggle I face I feel your
Strength dwelling in me
If you got my back, and we gather
two
or three,
*There too God will also be*

I vow to hold you to the principles of
Our ancestry
*"Leave no sister behind"*
I will pull you up when you are down
I will help you to **face your past**
**By acknowledging your future**

Together or in a bunch
There is nothing too difficult for us to
Bear
You are my sister
Your load is my load
Our burdens we will share

Sister, hold my hand, and you grab her hand,
And I will grab her hand over here
And together we will march forward accountable
For one another
*You are not heavy*
**You are my sister**

Roberta Sonsaray White
2-22-03

# My Sister, my best friend

*Used to wonder how many people were so blessed*
*With a wonderful sister who encourages them to be their very best*
*Tried to find the words to convey*
*My admiration for a love so true*
*Stood tall before many and few*
*Sis, I am what I am because I am loved by you*

*Disagreed with you many times*
*Only to discover that what you told me was right*
*Wanted to pave my own way*
*May have seemed to leave your side*
*But I carry you where ever I reside*
*A friend you are to me, and a sister you will always be*

*Always saw the light within*
*Forsook your friends in order to see me through*
*I thank God in heaven for you*

Danced all night and sometimes during the day
Always determined to make sure Lil' Sis was okay
Extended your hard love and life lessons to me
If it were not for you
"Ms. White" would not be

Molded me from the clay of Mom and Papa
Shaped me into my own person
Allowed me to experience trial and error
At the end of every challenge you were there
Cheering loudest above all voices
Letting the world know I'm your choice
All the days of my life it's your voice I hear
You are my shield of comfort when no one else cares
Bridgette, I thank you for loving me
You did not have to but you did

You stand in my shadow
Many will never know
Of this great Sister who loves me so
No way possible could I stand alone
You are my foundation, it's your hand I hold
Oh wind beneath my wings
Listen to my words
I am what I am because you love me.

Roberta Sonsaray White / August 13, 2003

# Mabel's Love

She loved with her whole heart:
Never judged a soul
She trusted so many men
Had to let a few go because of their stronghold
She believed in them
This is a tribute to my mother, it's called "Mabel's Love"

No woman ever loved humankind so
Was always quick to let you know
The depth of her heart, when she loved you, even if it hurt you
She was honest because she wanted you to fly
I know it is her love that keeps me high
On life with all of its uncertainties
If it weren't for her love, I would never be
This poem is called "Mabel's Love"

Now you know a little bit about how she loved me
But let me tell you how she loved thee, her man
Mabel was faithful in her loving
Always saw the best
Knew in her heart she deserved more

But was always willing
To test the perimeters of her loving sphere
And when warned by her people
Her heart would let the man she loved live inside of her
Both physically and mentally, soulfully, and kissily
Mabel loved the loving and the loveless
Sad thing, sometimes Mabel never received a loving kiss
Mama loved him who did not know how to love in return
This poem here is called Mabel's Love

One day God connected Mabel with a loving man
The love Mabel thought she knew could not compare
To the love this brother gave her, yes he took her there
Taught her how to cook and clean
Prior to him, and after men always called her, "Mean"
But he loved her

Took her from the streets
To live on a hill
Knew of her past, loved her children, and cared for her still
Not because she was a beauty Queen, but because she loved
With the heart of God

From the love of this woman and man
Came a woman who loves like
She & He
From their marriage union came me
This poem is called "Mabel's Love"

Roberta Sonsaray White
9-16-03

# *Master Copy*

Xerox created the copy machine
Because everyone in this world wants to be like me
Imitated, duplicated
Of course, why not
I am the master copy which means
I get clicked on a lot

Mini-mes in this world trying to cramp my style
Know it is my greatness you want
Not your original profile

Is that me in the mirror you're looking in?
Oh, it's my spiting image, my imaginary twin
Click me once, click me twice
Click me three times, for I'm three times as nice

I am the master, make a copy of me

Roberta Sonsaray White
10-30-03

# COURAGE TO
# BELIEVE

## I Corinthians 10[7]

[13] You have never been tempted to sin in any different way than other people. God is faithful. He will not allow you to be tempted more than you can take. But when you are tempted, He will make a way for you to keep from falling into sin.

How great are you? How great am I? Is it true that I can do all things through Christ who strengthens me? If you are uncertain about how to respond to these questions, perhaps your journey will take a little longer; continue reading, the answers are acquired on the journey. But, if you can stand confidently on what you have experienced up to this point, then you know the answer the each of these questions. One, you are as great as you believe you are. Two, I am great because God made me and the Holy Spirit saves me. Three, I can do all things through Christ who strengthens me. God has given each of us an infinite amount of power. When we ask for little, God is offended. God, the Maker of all things great and small, does not specialize in minimal blessings. In God's eyes, nothing is too good for us. Therefore, we must believe that we can have everything all the time. We serve a God who blesses us while living in sin and increases our blessings when we live according to the Divine plan designed for our individual lives.

Having the *courage to believe* is a humble gesture. Now that we are aware of our greatness, we must bow our heads even more. We owe God because God chose us first. Yet while we were deep in sin

God sent Jesus into the world to save us for God knew that we would reach a point in our journey where we would turn from many of our evil ways. As humans, we are bound to sin because we were born into sin. The blessing is that God knows us and is aware of our nature. However, even in our sinfulness, God expects us to believe that we are salvageable. Grace makes us whole.

In this section, you will experience humility and a shift in choices: from worldly to Godly in twenty-six poems.

## Luke 1[8]
[37] For with God nothing will be impossible

# *Unworthy*

I know I am not worthy of the gifts (love) God has for me
But He has taught me that He will provide my needs
if I just stand still

I know that I do not deserve His grace
Twenty-odd years later I realize that if I do not have faith I will never
See His face

I know that I am not worthy of receiving Heaven's key
Somewhere I read or it was said
That if I get down on bended knee, confess my faith,
run my race then I will
receive
The key

I know that God's amazing grace requires no assistance from me
But I believe that by helping others,
I help the Father, you see?

In spite of myself God still loves me.

Roberta S. White
7-14-02

# *Faith is . . .*

Like an eagle:
those who have it fly
High

Like tires on a car: though it hits bumps it keeps on rolling

Like dreams: invisible to the human eye, but complete in the
mind's eye

Like a lover: sometimes you will question its whereabouts, just
to learn that it is always with you

Like a test:
No matter how much you study, sometimes you have to fail in
order to learn that there is more to it than the notes (Bible) can tell

Like Jesus Christ:
It can only live and manifest itself in the heart of a believer

Roberta Sonsaray White
7-21-02

# This Solemn Plea

Oh Lord, that You would provide all my needs,
That You would lift me when I am low,

## Comfort me when I am lonely

I beg of You a second chance to do Your will
I failed to do my very best the first time,
I come to You now with my head bowed before You
In Your word, You confirmed that if I ask in faith it shall be given to me
Therefore I ask that you will bless me indeed so that I may shine for You
    this time

Let Your will be done that my burdens will be no more
Lord, I trust in You, and stand on Your word

Thank You for blessing me,
Thank You for a second chance,
Thank You for success granted through the Holy Spirit

Amen

—R.S. White 7/20/02

# This Little Prayer

*Creator God, Almighty, Wonderful, Powerful God,*

**I thank You for blessing me**
*I thank You for my challenges for I know they will make me stronger*

*Lord, I ask that You continue to fight my battles; I am not strong enough to win on my own*

*Great Redeemer, I ask that You walk before me to clear a path of peace for my journey*
*And Lord, please forgive all that I have failed to do for You*

*Merciful One, I thank You again for blessing me indeed.*

*Amen*
—R.S. White 7/20/01

# For The Child With No Mother

*Gracious soul, child of God*
*The Lord is with you today*

*Though you may be feeling down and out,*
*May you feel God's spirit I pray*

*Days will pass and you may feel alone,*
*But know in God's kingdom you have a home*

*A mother's love is rare and true*
*Though mommy's not available*
*God will see you through*

*Ain't it good to know that in Jesus you have a friend*
*Not for a moment,*
*But throughout the eternal end*

*Somebody prayed and is praying for you,*
*Darling child*

*Know that in God's time you will be washed*
*Anew . . .*

*The mother you need is God who lives within*
*You*

R. S. White
5-12-02
Written on Mother's Day
at Emory United Methodist Church

# Give Him the Praise

Waking up this morning, I knew
That everything would go my way,
I showered, got dressed, and
Grabbed my keys from the top of a bookshelf
Yet, I did not spend a second
On my praying knees

As the day progressed, I was filled
With joy, love, and hope
"Darn, my nail chipped," I griped
Yet, I did not praise my Creator

"Oh, well," I thought
I'm blessed, no need to be stressed."
At least I call on Him in times of need

Like a thief in the night
My day did not end all right
One disaster led to another
When least expected, the Creator took me to meet my brother
Lying in an alley
Stabbed many times he said, "Pray for me"

Suddenly, the Lord took his soul and they left

On this day I learned quite a bit:
Do not start your day without acknowledging God's gifts

R.S. White
3/26/00
Written at Clair Memorial UMC in Omaha, NE

# God Gave Me the Wind

I knew that it was time when the
Breeze swept across my ear;
When the breeze swept my ear
I knew it was time

Cottony sweet, the gentle wind was my treat;
Powerful enough to send the sound
Of my mother's voice
Yet, clear enough for God to say, "It's time"

In this hour of my time, God has led me to sunshine
And the rain falls at my feet never
To touch the crown of my head

Shining Fame, Roberta, a name, but would
I be as sweet by another name?

No longer awaiting, just anticipating
The greatness God has for me,
I worship
He anoints me
It's Time!

Roberta S. White
4-1-01
—inspired by God's promise to lead me to my destiny

# Magical Discipline

Twinkle, twinkle little star
I pray upon your shining beam
That you will honor my request today;
That you will show me God's way
Oh how I often get side-tracked by worldly distractions
I now realize that I need your strength to keep me from going under

Oh shining star so far up in the sky
Let you magical light shine on me no matter where you are

My request you know, my dreams we share, but without discipline,
nothing will bring me success
I need you forever to shine on me
Thank you for hearing my discipline plea

Amen

—R.S. White 7/20/01

# Live Life in Simple Sentences

## Period!
Yesterday is history, closed and ended.
Today is a new beginning full of life, love and means by which
to live
A broad future stands before me bright as the morning sun
I find comfort in knowing my life has just begun.

No longer concerned about the pessimist;
My life has upward view
No longer worried about those people who never spent time
with me;
God is all I need
No longer led by the threats of abandonment
Cause motivation drives me to believe that I ain't seen nothing yet.

Today is the day my life begins anew,
Life, love, and means by which to live are true!
All that I want, need and desire belongs to me
Today my visions and dreams spring into reality.

R.S. White
7-19-01

# Thankfulness for Encouragement

On this day, Creator God,
Go before me and pave the way
Make my transgressors to lay rest at Your feet;
Let no negative comments keep me from performing deeds.
Oh, I thank You for loving me through and through;
For keeping me lifted when others tried to pull me down
Merciful, Omnipotent One, thank You for bringing peace out of
chaos,
For Christian love untold,
Thank You for loving me, and strengthening me to be **bold!**

*Amen*

R.S. White 7-18-01

# If PawPaw Could

Grandpa used to tell Mama a story 'bout when he was a Child
How he and his brothers, his mother, and father
Received a ham covered in maggots
Down their chimney
How poor and hungry they were
And how he being an older brother,
Washed the ham for their eating

Mama used to tell me stories
Of selling Omaha Stars
With Her older brother
To purchase bread, and grease, and bacon
She did not tell of the bacon,
But how they rubbed their
Bread in it for the flavor and
Hopes of nourishment

Mama used to tell me about her one outfit
And bobby socks
And sharing a bed with several siblings
In a house with no bath tub,
But a wash sink

*Mama told me how she hustled to*
*Provide for her younger siblings*
*How she'd give the shirt off her back*
*To keep the little ones from being attacked*

*If Grandpa did, and Mama could, I know I can*
*Still not having all I want*
*But equipped with the genetics of*
**Survival**
*I can and will make it*
*I know how to rub a stick to a rock for heat*
*How to scrub floors, pots, and pans*
*I learned how to read and write*
*And I know how to pray that God*
*Carry me through the night*

*With all of my history*
*The support of my foundation*
*And a legacy of survival skills*
*I can and will make it*

*If Grandpa could, and Mama did,*
*I know I can.*

Roberta Sonsaray White
2-1-03
In remembrance of my mom and in dedication to my Grandpa

# *And I Wanna Thank You*

*No one on the face of the earth can tell about my journey
Better than I
No one on earth can really convey the empowerment given
Unto me through every joy, every cry
No one knows how at peace I am today,
And I wanna thank you
For Allowing God to use me in a special way*

*If someone would have told me of the
Blessings I would receive
I never would have believed
That God would bless one woman with gifts
To sustain those in need,
To encourage,
And to be encouraged by His miraculous ability
To make something out of nothing,
Nevertheless, I am grateful that the Creator chose me
And I wanna thank you
For allowing God to use me in a special way*

*I never really understood the beauty*
*Of love until I encountered a personal relationship with Christ*
*I never understood how one could be so content with being*
*A teacher, mother, and wife,*
*But God made my life this way*
*Because I was obedient when He*
*Led me to disciple folk unto Him*
*And I wanna thank you*
*For helping me to be a blessing in a special way*

*I wanna thank you for praying for me*
*I wanna thank you for loving me just as I am*
*I wanna thank you for understanding that God needs me elsewhere*
*right now*
*I wanna thank you for not asking when, why or how,*
*I just wanna thank you for letting God be God all by Himself*

*I Wanna Thank You*

In Memory of Mrs. Jessie Troy
By
Roberta S. White
8-11-02

# Stronger Than Tears

Lord, I know that I am stronger than these tears
If it were not so You would not have seen me through all these years
I know You are not ready to lead me home; You have a purpose
for my life that slowly, I am growing to know
You never raised me to depend on a man so I know that with
these two feet, on your word, I can stand
You keep surrounding me with people who tell me my worth; I
believe these messages are from you, so why do they not always work?
Lord, I pour my heart out to You and wonder if I sinned against
You so bad that You would condemn me to mediocrity
I am strong, Lord God, in You and Your Word; I became weak
though I knew full well that I was sinning against You
Lord, I am weak; right now I can not see my way
Let me turn this matter over to You so that You may have Your way
Creator, cleanse my heart that I may be pure
Submerge me in Your Holy Spirit so that a
protective veil will adorn me
Lord, I can not take back yesterday,
But today I ask that You will keep me from going astray.

Lord God, I am too blessed to stress the mess in my life.
Please place Your hand on my body to remove all anxiety
I need You to heal me from the crown of my head, down to my
heart, and even to the bottom of my feet, help me to understand
that You are all I need.
Lord, I am stronger than tears

Roberta S. White
11-8-02

# After the Storm

After the storm comes sunshine and rain
After the storm there is no pain
After the storm all sorrows are gone
After the storm, it won't be long.

After the storm celebration comes
After the storm people jump up and run
After the storm we forget to tithe
After the storm tell this old world good by

Then the storm rolls in again
Then the peace no longer settles in
Then such a mess arrives
Then there is suffering because of forgetting why
Then God elects to show some grace
Then, and only then do we see God's face

The storm rolls out, the spirit rolls in
The storm rolls out, and there is wholesomeness again

Roberta S. White
4-3-03

# *Luck*

Ever wonder where I got my luck?
Well, I changed a dollar into five nickels, two quarters, two
dimes, and a nickel
Took a nickel, plucked it far
Nickel jumped up, flew high, hit a car, sailed through the sky,
and passed the daily drivers right on by
"Ka-Plunk!" It landed in a near by pond
Pond's splash made a "Blop" in my front lawn
Then the wind drove me to the sea
To get a whiff of the air God created just for ME
With moisture comforting me, I strolled
By the pond to see a shiny old nickel, heads up, staring back at ME

Roberta S. White
4-17-03
(Dulles International Airport)

# *I AM*

I may not be all that you want me to be,
But I am all that God needs me to be.

I may look shabby to you on the outside,
But God gave me a heart of gold on the inside.

I may spring forth from a family rooted in issues of fornication,
adulteration, procrastination,
Alienation, and discrimination,
But I am chosen by God to do a new thing here on earth.

I may not be your ideal candidate for the job,
But I am God's appointed.

Back in the day I was a hooting, hollering, trouble causing child,
But today I am using that same voice to praise my Savior loud!

I may have been a poor example of my people,
But I now work to see that all humankind are created equal.

I am the blessings of generations past, faced with challenges,
heartaches and pain
Strong enough to deplete my ability to last.

Because God is and I am not, I stand.
I stand firm knowing that I am
Following a legacy of leaders.
I stand firm on the promises of my Lord.
I may not be and yes, I once was.
But by the grace of God, I am no longer what I used to be.
Because God is and I am not, I am favored by my Savior a
whole, whole lot!
I am the blessing of generations past.

Roberta Sonsaray White
5-31-03

# Cry For Me No More

Carry me on home, Dear Lord, for my weary feet are tired
I have walked in this cold and lonesome world many days
There were times when I felt as if no one cared as if I was alone.

When I called on my friends, no one answered
*I looked to my family to help ease my worries and my cares*
They too could not reach Me
When I called on my Father which art in Heaven He
Released my pressure and washed all my cares away
He took my hand and led me to a better way.
He assured me that I would trouble no more.
Then my Savior carried me through Heaven's open door.

Cry for me no more for I am in a better place.
I am with people who listen, comfort, and live by God's grace
I know that in my new home my friends and family care for
Me
This is God's will, now you can do as you please
If you ever feel a gentle breeze blow pass your ears,
Know that it is the breath of my love
For I will **always** keep you near.

Roberta Sonsaray White
8-99

# *Yesterday*

Yesterday, I almost gave up:
I felt hopeless and in despair,
Kept telling myself that no one cared

Yesterday, I almost took myself out:
I thought about all of what I didn't have,
All I wish I had
And the future seemed so bleak

Yesterday, I almost ran away:
I wanted to run from the reality that
Trials and tribulations come,
Wanted to run, grab a gun, and shoot myself far, far away from here

Yesterday, I almost forgot my past:
I focused so hard on the moment
So hard that all of my dreams began to fade away
Forgot about how I overcame before,
Forgot that there is nothing new in store
Didn't remember that what is has always been
And someday soon will come again

Yesterday, I almost forgot my calling:
Still fighting to live my own way,
Always trying to convince myself that my way is okay
Even after I analyze my situation, notice repeated habits,
And bits of procrastination
But I blocked these things out to see what I want to see

Yesterday, I almost forgot about today:
A new day filled with hope
Another chance to live freely, obediently, and according to the
Master's will
I was running so fast I failed to realize that my speed would get
me here; to the very place I was trying to avoid
So I kept running, and running, and running until I lost breath
I ran so hard, until there was no more running in me left
Tired and out of breath . . .
I stand and remember yesterday in order to make it through
today!

Roberta S. White
October 23, 2003

# The Eye of A Needle

Lord, make me so thin that I can slide through the eye of a needle
Remove all my burdens, problems, and those things that weigh
me down heavily
Creator snatch me from sin
That she may not steal my breath
Lord, dehydrate my body of lack, pain, and stress
Jesus, make me so thin that I glide through the eye of a needle

No more worries have I now
For this new cleansing I have found
The directions read, "Cast your cares on me. Take my yoke,
then walk away slim and free"
Best thing is, for this cure there is no fee
And from life's stress, I can walk away: slimmer, trimmer, and
ready to serve

I know this may sound bold to you
But God has instilled in me the nerve and courage to ask and receive
So I figured, "Why be heavy burdened when I can be full of praise?"
Even in my going through, Lord, help me to worship you
Just when life seems to bring me problems anew
Keep me fit, for through the eye of a needle, I must always be
able to pass through.

Roberta Sonsaray White
11-25-03

# I Can Stand

Used to wonder if I can stand
I wobbled along the way
Never knew how blessed I am
I had to test my fate
Always wanted something more than what was in my face
So I stopped and started listening to what my Savior had to say

Every now and then
I get brushed over to the side
It is at this point that I check myself and fine-tune my focus on God

After years of wobbling, crawling, and walking, I can finally stand
No matter what you've heard
Challenges test your ability to be a God fearing boy, girl,
woman, or man
When faced with faith and prayer on bended knee
Anything is possible; your goals will all be reached

Just stand!

Roberta Sonsaray White
6-8-03

# *Rejoice*

Do not cry over yesterday
For if you cry over yesterday, you will miss the blessings of today

Do not wish that you were or ponder what you could have been
Rejoice in what you are and shall soon become

Do not marvel over the gifts of others
Thank God for your blessings; thank your father and your
mother
Despite what they have or have not given you
Be grateful for all that the Creator allowed them to do

Do not sit with a mournful face
Understand that people come & people go,
And that no one can take your place

Do not ask the question, "Why Me"
Rather, thank the Heavens for the blessings and challenges that be

Do not turn your back on a needy women, girl, boy, or man
Lend them your heart, a prayer, some love, and a helping hand

Everyday of your life, live to the fullest
At the end of each day put an exclamation point on your life!
If there is work to be continued, write a message on your heart
that says so,
But deny malice, envy, regret, and shame to follow you; to make
you feel that you are to blame.
Grow, live, learn, share, and give
Give, live and never regret
Just Live!

RS White
6-17-03

# *Through It All*

## (A poem for Grandma)

Without a shadow of a doubt, the Lord carried me through
many tough times.
There were many days when I had to get on my knees in order
to carry on.
But through it all I remained faithful.

On my journey through this ever-changing world, I have seen
many faces, and even more situations.
And through it all I was loved.

Holding the riches of a loving husband, eleven beautiful
children, grandchildren and great grandchildren, without a
doubt I was always loved.

With every breath I took, every move that I made, I was well
aware that my way had already been paved.
Therefore, I leave you with these words of peace:
In this heart of mine from beginning to end, I carry the love for
family and friends.  Please do not grow weary in my physical
absence; for there is a better place where we will all someday
meet.  And if you ever feel that there is no way you can carry on,
just think about all the blessings God gives.

Roberta Sonsaray White
1-2000

# Ticket Out

I... got this one ticket to get me out of da ghetto
It's a ticket that only I possess
This here ticket gonna take me far, far away from here,
Yet, I will remain here, in debt to my people forever

I'm gonna go to Hollywood and sit with the stars
And when I finish,
I'm coming back to the District to talk to my people
I want to remain as an equal
But this here ticket, this one ticket, gonna get me out of da ghetto

Don't get me wrong, I like being here
But I know that God gonna move me far, far away from here
I mean I'm down for the struggle and will always write about
the cause
But right now I'm gonna write my way out of da ghetto

I'm taking every struggle, every blessing, every discriminatory act
done unto me and gonna share it with the world
I'm gonna tell my story, my Mama's story,
and the story of my Papa long gone
You see, I got one ticket and this here ticket gonna
get me out of the ghetto

Been thinking
And come to a conclusion that I owe no one an apology
for what I'm doing
You see, we all come to this world with gifts and talents
Some use them, others abuse them and many more lose
them for lack of usage
But me, I got one ticket, and I'm gonna write my
way out of the ghetto; gonna set me free

I know running free will have its challenges,
but it's nothing I can't handle

Heck, if you lived on my street you'd be confident enough to
know that every odd can be beat
My middle name should have been "Defeat" for I have survived
insurmountable odds
Not by my own means, all credit goes to God
for making me strong.

God gave me a song to sing
And I'm gonna sing it everywhere I go
Cause I got one ticket and I'm gonna use it every chance I get

Well, my train is here and I must go
Just wanted to share my ticketmony to let you know
That there is hope in the hood
Hold onto your ticket
The train is coming
And before it departs, you must get on board.

Roberta Sonsaray White
7-16-03

# Endnotes

## Acknowledgments

[1]  Matthew 25:40
*The Spiritual Formation Bible,* New Revised Standard Version copyright?
1999 by The Zondervan Corporation.

## Introduction

[1]  Matthew 5:15
*The Holy Bible,* New International Version copyright © 1973, 1978, 1984
by International Bible Society.
*The Holy Bible,* New King James Version copyright © 1994 by Thomas
Nelson, Inc.

[2]  *The American Heritage Dictionary.* 3rd ed. 1994.

[3]  Jeremiah 29:11
*The Spiritual Formation Bible,* New Revised Standard Version copyright ©
1999 by The Zondervan Corporation.

## Section Introductions

### Conflicts:

[1]  Galatians 5:16-18
The Holy Bible, New International Version copyright ©1973, 1978, 1984 by International Bible Society.

[2]  Jonah 3:8
The Holy Bible, New Living Translation copyright © 1996 by Tyndale Charitable Trust.

### Realization:

[3]  1 Corinthians 14:12
The Holy Bible, New Living Translation copyright © 1996 by Tyndale Charitable Trust.

[4]  Matthew 7:12
The Holy Bible, English Standard Version copyright © 2001 by Crossway Bibles.

### Respect:

[5]  Matthew 7:6
The Holy Bible, New King James Version copyright © 1994 by Thomas Nelson, Inc.

[6]  1 Corinthians 4:3
The Holy Bible, New International Version copyright © 1973, 1978, 1984 by International Bible Society.

### Courage to Believe:

[7]  1 Corinthians 10:13
The Holy Bible, New Life Version copyright © 1969 by Christian Literature International.

[8]  Luke 1:37
The Holy Bible, New King James Version copyright © 1994 by Thomas Nelson, Inc.